History At Home

Finding Out About Your Family History

Nick Hunter

Raintree is an imprint of Capstone Global Library Limited, a company incorporated in England and Wales having its registered office at 7 Pilgrim Street, London, EC4V 6LB – Registered company number: 6695582

www.raintreepublishers.co.uk
myorders@raintreepublishers.co.uk

Text © Capstone Global Library Limited 2015
First published in hardback in 2014
The moral rights of the proprietor have been asserted.

Edited by Catherine Veitch and Gina Kammer
Designed by Steve Mead and Peggie Carley
Picture research by Mica Brancic
Production by Helen McCreath
Originated by Capstone Global Library Ltd
Printed and bound in China by RR Donnelley Asia

ISBN 978 1 406 28151 4

18 17 16 15 14
10 9 8 7 6 5 4 3 2 1

British Library Cataloguing in Publication Data
A full catalogue record for this book is available from the British Library.

Acknowledgements
We would like to thank the following for permission to reproduce photographs:Alamy: Don Smetzer, 21, Homer Sykes Archive, 13, Marc Macdonald, 16, Wildscape/Tony Morris, 18; Getty Images: Archive Photos/Fotosearch, 22, Blend Images/KidStock, cover, Hulton Archive/Topical Press Agency, 20, kali9, 14, New York Daily News Archive/Ed Giorandino, 19, NoDerog, 17, Popperfoto, 24, Universal History Archive, 25, WireImage/Samir Hussein, 26; iStock: Ekely, 8, Lisa Valder, 7, Mark Bowden, 5; Newscom: ZUMA Press/Ana Venegas, 28, ZUMA Press/Michael Goulding, 23; Shutterstock: Blend Images, 9, Jeff Kinsey, 27, Monkey Business Images, 6, Rob Marmion, 11, Roberto Zilli, 4; SuperStock: 15, Blend Images, 29

Every effort has been made to contact copyright holders of material reproduced in this book. Any omissions will be rectified in subsequent printings if notice is given to the publisher.

All the Internet addresses (URLs) given in this book were valid at the time of going to press. However, due to the dynamic nature of the Internet, some addresses may have changed, or sites may have changed or ceased to exist since publication. While the author and publisher regret any inconvenience this may cause readers, no responsibility for any such changes can be accepted by either the author or the publisher.

Blackpool Council

Please return/renew this item
by the last date shown.
Books may also be renewed by
phone or the Internet.

Tel: 01253 478070
www.blackpool.gov.uk

Contents

Some words are shown in bold, **like this**.
You can find out what they mean by looking
in the glossary.

History and you

Everything that happened in the past is called history. Learning about the past can help us understand the world. We can learn about great events and famous people from history.

▲ Old buildings and other objects tell us about people who lived long ago.

History can also be about what has happened to you, your family, and the place where you live. There are lots of ways to find out about your family members and how they lived in the past.

▲ Older family members will be able to tell you about their lives before you were born.

Your family

Your family includes all the people related to you. Family members are close **relatives** such as your parents, brothers, and sisters.

▲ Families enjoy spending time together. They also share a family history.

Just as you have parents, so do your parents. These are your grandparents. Your parents and grandparents may also have brothers and sisters. Relatives who lived before you were born are called your **ancestors**.

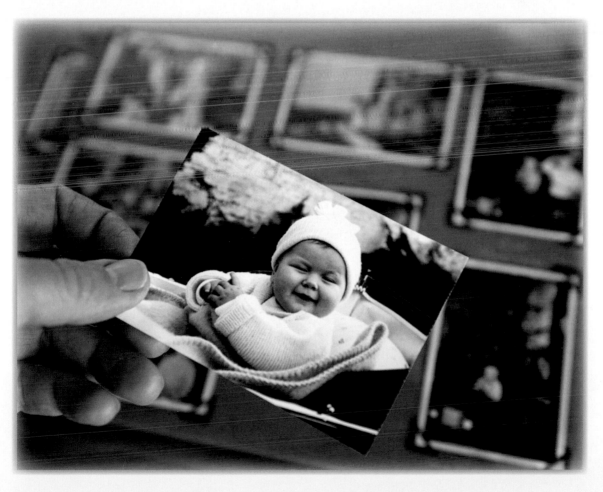

▲ Old family photos show you what your ancestors looked like.

Family history detective

To discover more, you need to look for clues like a **detective**. Ask your family members if they have any old photos, letters, and postcards. Names and addresses will help you to find information about your ancestors.

▲ Old letters and postcards can give lots of clues about your ancestors' lives.

You can use the names and details you find to search for information using a computer. There are lots of websites about family history. Ask a grown-up to help with this.

▲ You can also use a computer to type what you find out.

What is a family tree?

A **family tree** is a diagram that shows all the people who have been part of your family. It is called a family tree because it looks like a tree. It has branches spreading out from you at the bottom.

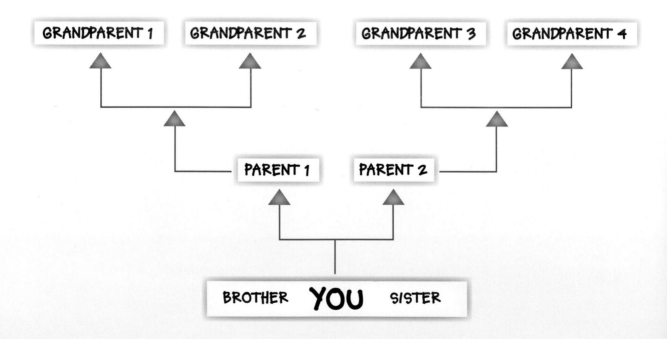

▲ This family tree shows three generations of a family: children, parents, and grandparents.

You have your own history to add to the family tree. Start by adding the date when you were born. You can also add your brothers' and sisters' names with their birth dates.

▲ Every year you celebrate your birthday on the date you were born.

Your parents

The next step is to discover more about your parents. You can ask them when and where they were born. Were they born somewhere very different from where you live now?

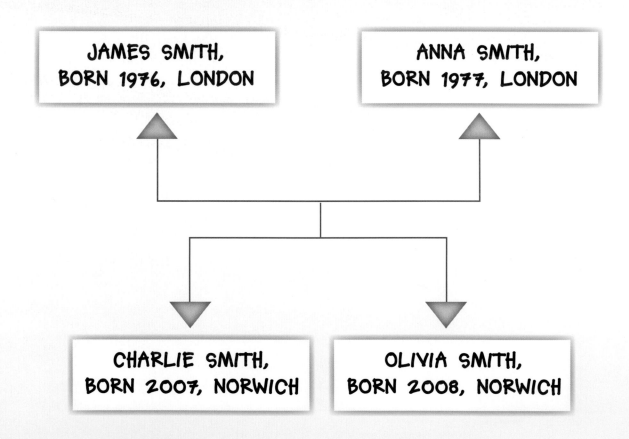

JAMES SMITH,
BORN 1976, LONDON

ANNA SMITH,
BORN 1977, LONDON

CHARLIE SMITH,
BORN 2007, NORWICH

OLIVIA SMITH,
BORN 2008, NORWICH

▲ This family tree now includes your parents.

You can find out much more about your parents by looking at old photos. Old photos show how different clothes looked in the past. Ask your parents how life has changed since they were children.

Do your parents ▶ remember clothes like these from the 1980s?

Grandparents

Your grandparents probably know more than anyone else about your family's past. They may be able to tell you about ancestors who died before you were born.

▲ Ask your grandparents if you can record their stories about your family.

Life has changed a lot since your grandparents were young. Fifty years ago, there were no home computers or mobile phones.

▲ What did your grandparents' homes and families look like when they were children?

Important documents

The government **records** some of the most important dates in our lives. A birth **certificate** shows when someone was born. It also includes the names of his or her parents.

▲ Birth certificates can tell you more about your family's history.

As you go further into the past, you will be finding out about relatives who are no longer alive. You should include in your notes the dates when they died. You may be able to find an **official** death certificate.

▲ Gravestones mark where people are buried.
  The dates when they died are carved on the stones.

Public records

Governments keep official records such as birth and death certificates. Churches and other organizations often have records going back hundreds of years.

▲ You can find some records on your computer, but you may have to visit a library or record office.

Censuses list all the people living in a particular house or area on a certain day. A census is taken every 10 years. Old census returns can tell you about your ancestors and where they lived.

▲ This census taker is asking questions to help complete a census form in 1960.

Local family

Has your family lived in the same town for a long time? You can find out more about your family's connections to your local area. Your town probably looked very different in the past.

▲ Can you find your family's home on an old photograph? This old image shows homes in 1908.

Shops and businesses are often named after the people who started them. Look for your family name on local businesses or other buildings. Old books and documents may help with your search.

▲ This restaurant began as a meat packing business by the Schmidt family in 1886.

Family far away

Many families have moved to where they live now from distant countries. This is called **immigration**. You can use official records to tell you where your ancestors came from.

▲ Immigrants' names are recorded when they arrive in a new country.

Tracing your family tree may introduce you to relatives who live far away. They may even live on the other side of the world. You could ask a grown-up to help you write a letter or email to find out how their lives are different from yours.

▲ Today immigrants are welcomed to their new countries with ceremonies and official documents.

Historical events

Your family history could help you to find out about events in the past. Millions of people went to fight in wars during the 1900s. If your great grandparents are still alive, they may remember living during World War II, which ended in 1945.

▲ If your ancestors served in the **armed forces**, try to find photos or letters they sent.

Some families find that their ancestors lived through very difficult times. In the past, black people were taken from Africa as **slaves**. Some families discover that their ancestors were slaves.

▲ Slavery was common in the countries of the Caribbean and southern United States before 1865.

Famous family trees

Some family trees are already well known. Royal families can trace their ancestors back through a long line of kings and queens.

▲ The children and grandchildren of Queen Elizabeth II may one day become king or queen.

If you can trace your ancestors back a long way, you will discover hundreds of relatives. You could find that you have a famous ancestor. Maybe you are related to someone who is famous now.

▲ Could you be related to the president of the United States?

Your history project

It is important to keep records of what you learn from talking to people. You could record your interview or use pen and paper to take notes.

▲ If you record your interview, it will be easier to share with others.

You can use what you learn from talking to people to create a history project. Include old photos and things that you have learned from other books. You could share what you have learned with your friends and family.

▲ There are lots of sources you can use to learn about the past.

Find out more

Books

Be a Family Tree Detective (Who Do You Think You Are?), Dan Waddell (Walker, 2010)

My Family Tree Book (First Record Book), Catherine Bruzzone and Lone Morton (b small publishing ltd, 2006)

My Indian Family History (Family Histories), Vic Parker (Heinemann Library, 2007)

Websites

kids.familytreemagazine.com/kids/default.asp
A family tree resource for young people.

familysearch.org/learn/wiki/en/Family_History_Activities_for_Children:_3-11
This website is full of ideas for family history activities.

projectbritain.com/royaltree.htm
Visit this website to see the famous family tree of the British Royal Family.

Glossary

ancestor family member who lived in the past

armed forces organizations that defend your country and fight in war if needed, including the army, navy, and air force

census regular survey to count and gather information about people living in an area

certificate formal document that states a fact, such as a certificate proving someone's date of birth

detective person who uses clues to discover facts

family tree diagram that shows different generations and branches of a family

immigration when people move from the country where they were born to live in a new country

official something that comes from the government or another authority

record written document about something that happened in the past

relative someone from the same family

slave person who another person claims to own, keeping them captive and forcing them to work without pay

Index